The Little Witch's Book of Toys

by Linda Glovach

Prentice-Hall Books for Young Readers
A Division of Simon & Schuster, Inc.
New York

For George Cooke

Published by Prentice-Hall Books for Young Readers
A Division of Simon & Schuster, Inc.
Simon & Schuster Building
Rockefeller Center
1230 Avenue of the Americas
New York, New York 10020

10 9 8 7 6 5 4 3 2 1

Prentice-Hall Books for Young Readers is a
trademark of Simon & Schuster, Inc.
Printed in Spain

Library of Congress Cataloging-in-Publication Data

Glovach, Linda.
The Little Witch's book of toys.

Summary: The Little Witch gives instructions for
making toys and games from readily available materials.
1. Toy making—Juvenile literature.   2. Games—
Juvenile literature.   [1. Toy making.   2. Games.
3. Handicraft]   I. Title.
TT174.G59   1986   745.592   86-9416
ISBN 0-13-537879-6

Contents

INTRODUCTION

Where the Little Witch lives the winters are long and cold and she spends much of her time indoors with her friends. They keep busy by making their own toys. Some of the toys are for them to love and play with and to decorate their rooms with. But others they give away or put on display in school and at the library.

A toy you make yourself can be more fun than the expensive toys bought in stores, because making toys is as much fun as playing with them. The Little Witch and her friends save empty cereal boxes, tissue boxes, pieces of cardboard, and cardboard tubes from toilet paper and paper towels. They buy inexpensive craft materials such as poster paper, poster board, and poster paints. In this book they will show you how to make an Acrobatic Twirling Frog, a Bumpy Alligator, a Witch Roadster, and even a Robot. You can scare your friends with Monster Mitts and Claw Paws. In the last section of this book, the Little Witch tells you how to plan a Toy Workshop Sale and Party.

Remember, when you make a toy of your own, there is not another one exactly like it in the whole world. Use your own ideas and enjoy!

TOY WORKSHOP TIPS FROM THE LITTLE WITCH

1. Always get permission from your parents or a responsible adult before you start a project.

2. Scissors, staplers, and paints should be used carefully and with adult supervision.

3. Do not empty a box of cereal, cake mix, or tissues to make a toy unless you have permission to do so. Collect boxes for future toy-making sessions as they become empty.

4. When using paints, protect your clothing by wearing a smock or old clothes and cover the floor and tables with newspapers. Let paint dry before going on to the next step.

5. Clean up your work area after making toys, or set aside a special area for your own workshop.

6. Study the pictures in this book before you begin each toy until you understand how to make the toy. Look over the list of materials required to make sure you have all the materials you will need.

7. Remember—no toy has to come out perfect. Your toy should be your very own special work. You can give your toys any names you prefer, not just the ones suggested in the book.

FRIENDLY ANIMAL TOYS

Endangered Species Pets, and Animal Character Dolls

LEO THE LEOPARD (endangered species pets)

Some animals in the world, such as the tiger, leopard, lion, polar bear, seal, wolf, sea otter, and prairie dog, are endangered species. This means there aren't many of them left. In order to survive, they must be protected from their enemies and their natural homes must be saved. Many wildlife and nature groups are helping to protect these animals. The Little Witch and her friends make some of their own wildlife pets to remind themselves and others to help save the animals.

How to Make Leo

You need: a standard-size empty cereal-flakes box (10.5 or 18 oz.), or a similar-size box; at least two 12″ × 18″ sheets, and one 8″ × 1½″ strip of yellow construction paper; two 2¾″ × 2¾″ pieces and six 4″ × ¼″ strips of black construction paper; four 2¾″ × 2¾″ and two 2″ × 2″ squares of orange construction paper; black and green poster paint, glue, scissors, and stapler.

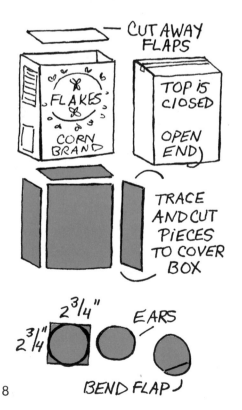

Cut away the flaps on the opened top of your cereal box, so your hand and arm can fit through it later. This will be the bottom of Leo, and the closed bottom will be the top of his head. Trace the outline of the front, back, top, and sides of your cereal box on yellow construction paper. Cut out the pieces and glue them on the sides, so they cover the entire box except for the bottom. Draw a circle on each 2¾″ × 2¾″ piece of black construction paper and cut out (see picture). Bend one edge of each circle in a ¼″ flap. Glue or tape the flap to top sides of box, as in picture.

Measure 2¼″ down from top of box and paint green eyes, about the size of half dollars. Outline the eyes in black and paint black pupils in them. Paint a pink triangle-shaped nose. Draw a full circle on each 2″ × 2″ square of orange paper and cut out. (Try tracing around a drinking glass or paper cup, if you have trouble drawing circles.) Glue one circle to each side of nose. Glue three 4″ × ¼″ strips of black construction paper to each circle. Paint some tiny dots on circles. Draw a paw on each 2¾″ × 2¾″ orange square and cut out (see picture). Paint black paw grooves. Make a ½″ flap on each paw. Staple two paws to bottom by flaps and glue two paws about 3½″ above bottom paws.

Round off one end of 8″ × 1½″ yellow tail strip with scissors. Tape other end of tail to back of box by a ½″ flap, attaching tail about 2½″ up from bottom of leopard. Paint black spots all over front, back, sides, and tail of Leo. Wear Leo and all your wildlife cereal box pets over your hand and arm to play act.

How to Make Leslie the Lion

You need: two 12″ × 18″ sheets of orange construction paper, four 2¾″ × 2¾″ and two 2″ × 2″ pieces of yellow construction paper, twenty 3½″ × ½″, six 3″ × ¼″ strips of yellow crepe paper, six 4″ × ¼″ strips of white construction paper or poster board, one 8½″ × ½″ strip of orange construction paper, ruler, paints, glue, and stapler.

All same as for LEO

2¾" x 2¾" EARS

NOSE CIRCLES 2" x 2"

WHISKERS 2¾"

PAWS 2¾" x 2¾"

SIX STRIPS TOWARD FRONT, SIX TOWARD BACK

FOUR STRIPS TO EACH SIDE

8" ½" Tail Like a Broom

Glue Flap Part

LESLIE LION and CUB

Cut off top flaps and cover the cereal box with orange construction paper, as you did for Leo. Make the ears as before, but use yellow construction paper. Paint on eyes, pink nose, and glue yellow circles next to nose. Glue three white whiskers over each circle. Cut paws out of yellow construction paper and staple and glue in place.

To make lion's mane, glue four of the yellow crepe paper strips to each side of box below ears. Glue only about ½" of each strip to box, so the rest hangs loosely. Glue six strips close together at top and front of box, so they hang forward, and glue six strips at the back, as in picture. Glue on extra strips for a thicker mane, if you like. Staple six 3" × ¼" strips to one end of the 8" × ½" tail. Glue 1" of the other end of tail to back of box by a tiny flap. To make Lion and Leopard Cubs, make them look just like the larger animals, but use smaller measurements. Save small, one-ounce cereal boxes. For ears and paws, use 1¼" × 1¼" squares of colored paper. Paint circles next to nose and whiskers. For the tail, use a 3½" × 1½" piece of construction paper. The crepe strips for the mane and tail fur should be 1½" × ¼".

SARAH THE BABY SEAL

Seals are also endangered wildlife. Some kinds of seals are hunted for their fur. The Little Witch knows a seal named Sarah. Sarah does tricks and is very tame. You can make a toy seal like Sarah.

You need: Two 9″ × 12″ pieces of gray or white craft felt (costs about 39¢ a sheet in a variety store), one 3″ × 1½″, one 8″ × 12″, and two 4½″ × 5½″ sheets of pink craft felt, six 3″ strings, paints, stapler, white glue, cotton, or rags.

Put two pieces of 9″ × 12″ felt together and round off the top corners with scissors. Staple sides and top—but not the bottom! Turn the felt inside out, so staples are inside. Paint two eyes about 1½″ down from top. Draw an oval on the 3″ × 1½″ piece. Cut out. Glue oval below eyes, as in picture. Paint on a black nose with two fishhook-shaped lines under it for a smiling mouth. Glue three strings to each side for whiskers.

To make fins, measure 2¼″ in from bottom of each 4½″ × 5½″ piece of craft felt. Mark a dot and from dot draw a diagonal line to each corner to make a triangle shape. Cut out on lines and round top corners with scissors as in picture. Staple fins to front of seal, 2″ up from bottom. For the tail fin, draw the same triangle shape on the 8″ × 12″ piece of craft felt. Glue tail fin to back of seal, 3″ up from bottom. Stuff seal with cotton, tissues, or rags, until it is about 1½″ thick. Staple bottom closed.

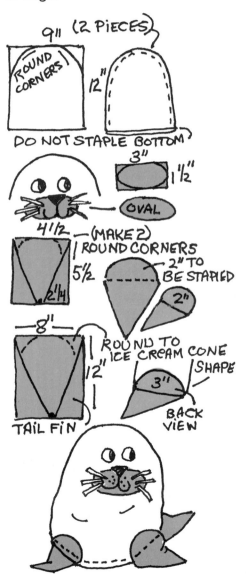

11

FRIENDLY FOREST UNICORNS

Unicorns are mythical beings, which means that they exist only in stories. Unicorns have only one long horn in the center of their foreheads. The Little Witch and her friend the Goblin saw one near the snowy forest where they live, so they decided to make their own Unicorns to play with. Nice Unicorn colors are pink, pale blue, white, lavender, light yellow, and sea green.

You need: an empty 18-oz. cylindrical oatmeal box (or a similar box from bread crumbs, potato chips, corn meal, etc.). Also, one 7¼" × 6¾" piece of pink or blue construction paper, one 4" × 4", one 8½" × 3¾", and two 4" × 2" pieces of yellow construction paper, one 12½" × 7" piece of construction paper in pink or any color you choose for your Unicorn. Also, two 6" × 3½" pieces of yellow or white construction paper, a 4½" × 3" piece of cotton batting, white glue, transparent tape, scissors, stapler, ruler, and paints.

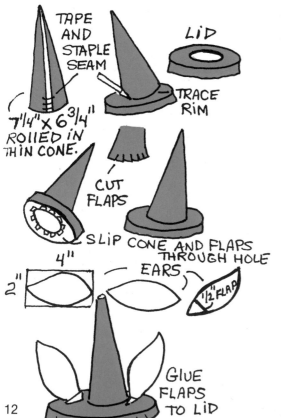

First make Unicorn's horn and ears. Take a piece of construction paper that is 7¼" wide by 6¾" high and roll it into a slim cone shaped like a church steeple. Trim excess at bottom so it is nice and even. Tape seam closed securely and put three staples near the base of the seam, as in picture. Trace rim of horn in center of oatmeal-box lid. Cut out circle. Cut several small ½" flaps around bottom of horn. Slip base of horn through lid and tape flaps underneath.

To make ears, draw one ear on each 4" × 2" piece of construction paper, as in picture. Cut out. Bend a ½" flap at one end of each ear and tape or glue flap to lid, one ear on each side of horn.

Paint lid pink or whatever color you have chosen for the 12½" × 7" piece of construction paper. Let it dry while you make rest of your Unicorn.

To make the muzzle, roll the 8½" × 3¾" piece of yellow construction paper, in a cylinder. Tape and staple seam closed (see picture). Trace the rim on the 4" × 4" piece of construction paper. Draw ½" flaps all around circle and cut out. Place this circle over one rim of the 8½" × 3¾" cylinder-shaped muzzle, as in picture. Bend flaps down and tape them to cylinder. Use clear tape or masking tape to cover flaps and then paint over them so they blend in with muzzle.

Trace the rim of the muzzle on the 12½ × 7" sheet of construction paper you will use to cover oatmeal box. Before tracing rim, measure 4½" in from right side and 1½" down on the sheet. Cut out circle carefully inside the lines, so muzzle will fit well. Cut flaps on end of muzzle and slip flaps through hole and tape them down carefully to other side of sheet. Don't rush.

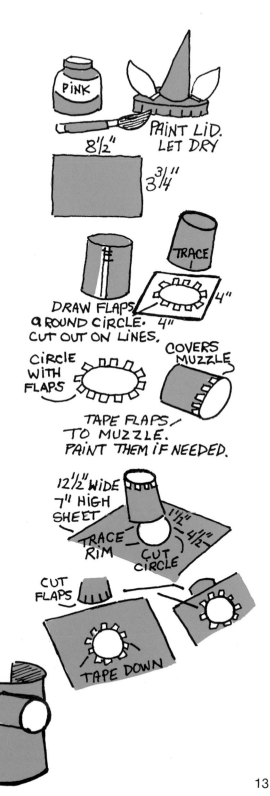

PINK

8½"

3¾"

PAINT LID. LET DRY

TRACE

DRAW FLAPS. a ROUND CIRCLE. CUT OUT ON LINES.

4"

4"

CIRCLE WITH FLAPS

COVERS MUZZLE

TAPE FLAPS TO MUZZLE. PAINT THEM IF NEEDED.

12½" WIDE 7" HIGH SHEET.

TRACE RIM

1½"

4½"

CUT CIRCLE

CUT FLAPS

TAPE DOWN

MUZZLE IN PLACE ATTACHED TO SHEET

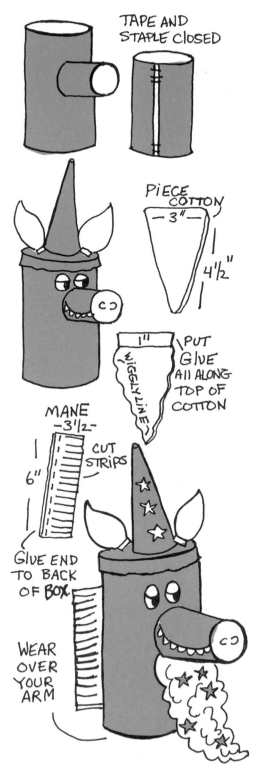

TAPE AND STAPLE CLOSED

PIECE COTTON
— 3" —
4½"

1"
WIGGLY LINE
PUT GLUE AII ALONG TOP OF COTTON

MANE
—3½—
6"
CUT STRIPS

GIUE END TO BACK OF BOX

WEAR OVER YOUR ARM

Now fit the sheet around the oatmeal box with muzzle in place, so it completely covers oatmeal cylinder. Tape seam tightly closed and put three staples at top. Paint eyes above muzzle, outline them in black and add black pupils. Paint a happy grin up sides of muzzle, with small, rounded teeth and two nostrils at front. Now you can put lid on box, if you like.

To make beard, cut a piece of cotton from a roll about 4½" long, 3" wide. With scissors cut a wiggly line up each side, as in picture. Spread a one-inch-wide band of glue across entire top of beard and spread a thin line of glue under muzzle. Glue beard to muzzle, as in picture.

To make mane, place the two 3½" × 6" pieces of construction paper together. Staple the two pieces together all along one side, as in picture. Cut 3" strips all along the other side at ¼" intervals to make the mane. Glue the stapled side of the mane to the Unicorn's back. Fluff out strips, if you like. Decorate beard with stick-on stars or glitter. Wear the Unicorn over your arm to play act, or display on a shelf in your room.

THE THREE COUNTRY BEARS

The three country bears are very easy to make. You can act out *Goldilocks and the Three Bears* and other stories with them. (You can use the Goldilocks doll described on page 33.) The Little Witch and her friend the Goblin use the Bears in the plays that they make up. You can do this, too.

You need: for each adult bear, one 3″ × 3″, two 1½″ × 1½″, one 4″ × 5″, four 1½″ × 3¾″ pieces of cardboard painted brown, one 4″ × 5″ piece of brown craft felt, two 6″ × 6″ pieces of fabric in the basic color and pattern you want for each Bear's nightshirt, two 5½″ pieces of pipe cleaners, paper fasteners, a roll of cotton batting, paints, scissors, ruler, stapler, and glue.

Mama and Papa Bear are made the same way, except Mama wears a different shirt. Draw a full circle on the 3″ × 3″ piece of cardboard and cut it out to make Bear's head. Draw a circle on each 1½″ × 1½″ piece of cardboard and cut out to make ears. Staple ears to top of head, as in picture. With scissors, round off corners of the 4″ × 5″ piece of craft felt. Trace form on the craft felt. Cut out form and glue it down to fit over the cardboard body. If you like, cut pieces of craft felt to fit and glue over ears. Paint yellow eyes the size of a penny on Bear and add black pupils. Paint the pink nose under eyes and the small fishhook-shaped mouth below nose.

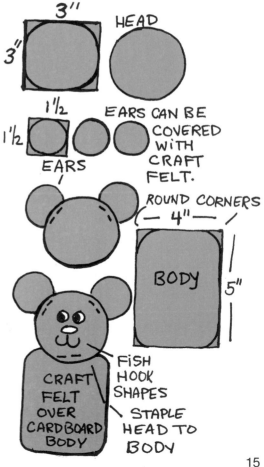

3″ · 3″ · HEAD

1½ · 1½ · EARS · EARS CAN BE COVERED WITH CRAFT FELT.

ROUND CORNERS — 4″ — BODY 5″

CRAFT FELT OVER CARDBOARD BODY · FISH HOOK SHAPES · STAPLE HEAD TO BODY

3¼"

1½"

ARMS
and LEGS
all THE
Same
SIZE

BE
SURE
TO LEAVE
BORDERS

6"x6" FABRIC.
TRACE BEAR'S BODY FORM.

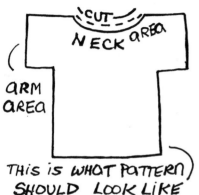

CUT
NECK AREA

ARM
AREA

THIS IS WHAT PATTERN
SHOULD LOOK LIKE

Make four arms and legs out of cardboard for each bear. Arms and legs should all be the same size, 1½" wide by 3¼" high. Round off corners on each piece. Attach arms to body by paper fasteners. Position fasteners ½" down from top of arms and legs and on Bear's body at top of shoulder, about ¼" in from edge, as in picture. If you have trouble putting a paper fastener in, punch a slight hole first on the cardboard, then put fastener through. An adult should help with it, especially going through craft felt.

To make nightshirt, you will need two pieces of 6" × 6" fabric in a color or pattern you like. Lay Bear over one of the pieces, with head, arms, and legs extending beyond the cloth. With marker gently trace Bear's form for a shirt. Outline the upper ¾ of Bear's arms and trace along body, but you must leave at least ½" border of fabric all along Bear's shirt, so you can staple this closed to the other piece later. Cut out and trace this same pattern again on the second 6" × 6" piece of fabric. Cut that out also. Don't forget to cut out the neck area. Place the Bear on one half of the nightshirt and cover with the other half.

Staple the seams closed along top of arms, underneath arms, and down body, as shown in picture. Use different material for Mama and Papa's nightshirts. You can use the same basic shirt pattern for Baby Bear. Paint buttons, stripes, patches, or flowers on shirts.

To make spectacles, for each Bear cut a piece of pipe cleaner about 5½" long. Roll each end in a circle and twist ends of pipe cleaner over circles, as in picture. Put glue all over one side of pipe cleaner and place above Bear's nose and over eyes. Glue some cotton balls to top and sides of Mama Bear's head for hair.

To make Baby Bear, copy directions for Mama and Papa Bear, but make everything smaller. For Baby Bear you will need pieces of cardboard painted brown. For the head, use a 2¼" × 2¼" piece of cardboard; for the body, use a 3" × 4" cardboard; for arms and legs, use two 1" × 2½" pieces of cardboard; and for the ears, you will need 1" × 1" pieces of cardboard. Make the nightshirt of two pieces of 5½" × 5" cloth. Don't add eyeglasses. The Bears' arms and legs are movable. Cut a slit up the center of the Bears' nightshirts, if you want them to be removable. You can make extra shirts if you want to.

2" (PATTERNS) ONE UNDER BEAR. ONE OVER BEAR

DO NOT STAPLE NECK AREA

DO NOT STAPLE BOTTOM

5½" PIPE CLEANER

TWIST END OVER circle

PAPA BEAR

MAMA BEAR

BABY BEAR

PATCHES

PUSS IN BOOTS

Puss in Boots, a very clever cat, went in search of food for Jack, his master, who was a poor miller's son. Along the way he met a King and a mean Ogre. Puss tricked the Ogre into turning himself into a mouse and then ate him. Then he invited the King to the castle and got his master married to the King's daughter, and they all lived happily in the castle. The Little Witch likes to make a Puss in Boots character doll.

You need: an 18-oz. round oatmeal box, one 4″ × 4″, two 1″ × 1″, one 5″ × 1″, and two 4½″ × 1¾″ pieces of cardboard painted light gray, and two 1½″ × 2″ pieces painted red, two 4½″ lengths of cardboard toilet-paper roller painted gray, one 12″ × 5″ piece of cloth of any color you like, 20″ of ribbon, one 8″ × 1″, and one 13″ × 1″ strip of white craft felt, one 5½″ × 2″, and one 2″ × 2½″ piece of blue construction paper, one 1½″ × 3″, and one 1½″ × 1½″ piece of yellow construction paper, paper fasteners, paints, scissors, stapler, ruler, and glue. Allow sufficient time for all painted pieces to dry.

Remove lid of oatmeal box and save. Draw a full circle on the 4″ × 4″ piece of cardboard, as in picture. Cut out. Draw triangle ear on each 1″ × 1″ piece. Cut out. Paint insides pink. Staple to top of head. Paint two nickle-size green eyes, a pink nose with fishhook-shaped mouth under it, and draw six whiskers. Staple head to oatmeal box, 1″ down from rim. Draw the fat hot-dog shape on each 4½″ × 1¾″ piece of cardboard. Cut out for arms. Have an adult punch a tiny hole on each side of box, 2½″ down from top, and punch a hole near top of each leg. Put a paper fastener through each hole and attach arms and legs through the holes on the box.

Cut tiny flaps all around the top of each toilet-paper cylinder. Bend the flaps and glue them to bottom of box. Use plenty of glue and hold cylinders in place for 5 minutes to let glue set. Staple the 20″ length of ribbon to the top of the 12″ × 5″ cloth for cape, with 4″ of ribbon extending out on each side, so you can tie cape around Puss. Round off one end of 8″ × 1″ felt for tail. Glue flat end of tail to back of Puss. Draw a circle on the 1½″ × 1½″ piece of yellow construction paper. Cut out. Paint a cross on it. Staple to top of 5″ × 1″ strip of cardboard to look like handle of sword. Round off bottom of sword. Draw an oval hat on the 2″ × 5½″ piece. Cut out. Cut a 2½″ slit in middle, just long enough to slip over cat's ears. Staple bottom of 2½″ × 2″ piece of blue construction paper above slit to form crown of hat. Draw feather on the 3″ × 1½″ piece of yellow construction paper. Cut out. Staple top of feather next to crown of hat. Wrap the 13″ × 1″ craft felt strip around cat's waist. Staple closed. Drape cape around cat's oatmeal-box shoulders and tie closed. Draw shape of boot bottom on each 1½″ × 2″ piece of red cardboard and cut out. Form a flap and tape to back of leg cylinders. Paint bottom of leg cylinders red to match boot bottoms. Slip sword in belt, hat over ears.

FLAPS 4½″ CYLINDERS
GLUE FLAPS UNDER BOX
TRIM TO EVEN

12″
4″ 4″
5″
CAPE

8″
1″ TAIL

SWORD
5″

1″

5½″
BLUE OR GREEN 1½″ 2″ 1½″

1½″
3″
FEATHER

2″ HAT
2½″ BLUE OR GREEN 2½″
SLIT

SLIGHTLY LOOSE BELT

13″×1 BELT

1½
RED 2″

CAT BOOT BOTTOMS

BOOTS

BEND AND TAPE. STAND BOOTS FLAT.

JEFF THE LONG-NECKED GIRAFFE

Here is an animal friend you can make in just a few minutes. You can act out stories while holding his cylinder body on your three middle fingers. Make one giraffe for each hand.

You need: an 11″ cardboard cylinder painted orange, (from paper towels, aluminum foil, etc.), one 4″ × 3¾″ piece of poster board painted orange, one 5″ × ¼″, one 1½″× 1″, and two ¼″ × 1¾″ pieces of orange construction paper, two 1¼″ lengths of pipe cleaner, six 2″ pieces of orange yarn or crepe paper, scissors, stapler, ruler, and paint.

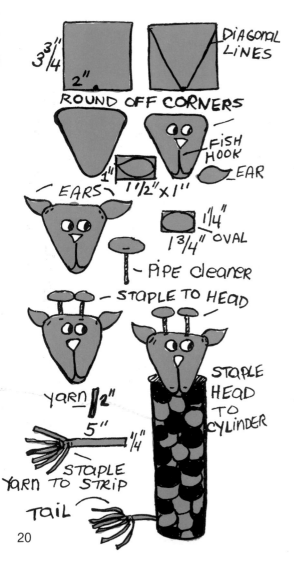

Measure 2″ up from one bottom end on the 4″ × 3¾″ piece of orange poster board. Mark dot. From dot draw diagonal line to each corner and cut out triangle shape. Round off edges with scissors. Paint penny-size green eyes outlined in black, a pink nose, and two fishhook shapes reaching to bottom dot. Draw a leaf-shaped ear on each 1½″ × 1″ piece of orange construction paper and cut out. Staple ears to top of head. Draw an oblong shape on each ¼″ × 1¾″ piece of construction paper and cut out. Staple each oblong to a piece of pipe cleaner. Staple pipe cleaners to top of head for horns. Staple Giraffe's head to top of cylinder. Staple a tuft of yarn to one end of the 5 × ¼″ strip of construction paper. Staple other end to back of cylinder for tail. Paint spots on Jeff.

ALL SORTS OF EASY-TO-MAKE TOYS FOR GIRLS AND BOYS

Frogs, Dragons, Alligators, Dolls, Robots, Witch Roadsters

ACROBATIC TWIRLING FROG

The Little Witch likes frogs. She has a pet frog named Ferdie. Watching Ferdie play gave her the idea for making an acrobatic twirling frog.

You need: an empty, standard-size tissue box (200 tissues), one 1½″ × 2½″ and four 1″ × 1¾″ pieces of cardboard painted green, a 3½″ length of a cardboard toilet-paper cylinder painted green, a full-length writing pencil (about 7½″ long), paper fasteners, stapler, ruler, scissors, paints.

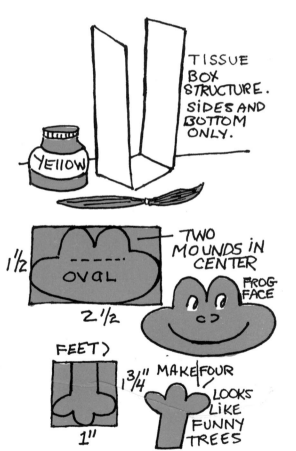

TISSUE BOX STRUCTURE. SIDES AND BOTTOM ONLY.

YELLOW

TWO MOUNDS IN CENTER

OVAL

1½

2½

FROG FACE

FEET ⟩

1¾″

3/4″ MAKE FOUR

1″

LOOKS LIKE FUNNY TREES

Stand the empty tissue box on end. Cut out front, back, and top piece, as in picture. Leave only the sides and bottom standing. Paint the box any bright color. Put the paint on thick. You may need three coats. You may want to paint your pieces the night before you are planning to make your frog, so the paint will have time to dry.

Draw the frog's head with two mounds in center extending 1½″ down from top on the 1½″ × 2½″ piece of cardboard. Then make a wide oval to complete head shape, as in picture. Cut out. Paint on eyes, nostrils, and wide smile with dark paint. Draw the four leg shapes, one on each 1″ × 1¾″ piece, to look like upside-down trees, as in picture. Cut out.

Attach frog's head by chin to top of toilet-paper roller, about ¼″ down from top. Trace the outline of the end of a pencil eraser in top center of one of the frog's legs. Then trace it on the other leg. Cut out the small circles (the pencil will go through these holes later). Attach each front leg with a paper fastener. Fasten front legs by the straight end, about ½″ down from the top of cylinder. Staple the other two legs to bottom, as in picture.

Raise the two front legs straight up over frog's head. Slip the pencil through one hole, then the other, so frog is hanging in center of pencil. Punch a hole (pencil-eraser size) 1½″ down from each top side of tissue box. Place pencil, with frog still attached into tissue box frame, as in picture. Slip point of pencil through one hole and eraser end through the other hole, so about 1″ of pencil will stick out on each end. Frog is attached to frame by pencil bar, like an acrobat. Paint stars, moons, and dots on box, and spots on frog. Twirl froggie over the bar.

CYLINDER

ATTACH HEAD HERE.

3½

ATTACH BY PAPER FASTENER

BACK VIEW

TRACE PENCIL ERASER IN CENTER

PAPER FASTENER

CUT OUT CIRCLES

ATTACH TOP LEGS TO SIDE TOPS.

STAPLE TWO, TO BOTTOM

PENCIL THROUGH HOLES

SIDE TO BACK VIEW

1½

HOLES ON SIDES OF BOX.

FROG TWIRLS AROUND BAR. PUSH HIM OVER IT. HE SWINGS BACK AND FORTH.

ALBERT THE ALLIGATOR

The Little Witch and Goblin make their very own pet alligator. An alligator is nice to have around the house, especially if you want to keep little brothers and sisters quiet. You can tie Albert to your bedpost or doorknob. If you want a female alligator, you might name her Alice and paint on pink spots.

You need: nine 6-oz. styrofoam cups, one 3½″ × 3½″, one 1½″ × 6″, and four 4″ × 3¾″ pieces of poster board or lightweight cardboard, one 3½″ × ¼″ strip of cardboard, 40″ of ribbon or string, paper fasteners, tempera or poster paints, ruler, tape, stapler, and scissors.

   Paint both sides of the poster board and cardboard pieces green. Let dry. Paint the outside of 9 styrofoam cups green, also. You may need two coats of paint, so it is a good idea to do this the night before the project day.

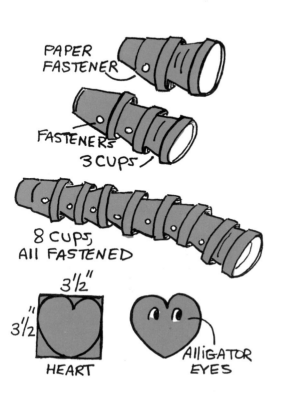

PAPER FASTENER

FASTENERS
3 CUPS

8 CUPS,
All FASTENED

3½″
3½″
HEART

Alligator
EYES

Look at the picture. Place one cup halfway inside the other and attach the two together at that point with a paper fastener stuck through both cups. Stick another cup halfway into the second cup and attach the same way, so you have three cups hooked together. Repeat this until you have 8 cups fastened together.
   Draw the heart shape on the 3½″ × 3½″ piece. Cut out for head. Paint a yellow eye with a black pupil in each mound. Bend a ½″ flap near the

pointed end of the heart. Staple the heart to the last styrofoam (ninth) cup (see picture). Paint a curved black mouth up each side of cup and paint the outline of pointed teeth under it. Staple 1″ of the 3½″ green strip inside this cup and staple 1″ of the other end of the strip to the first cup of the body. This will connect the heart-shaped head and jaw to the body, as shown in picture.

Draw a tall, thin triangle on the 1½″ × 6″ piece of poster board. Cut out. Form a ½″ flap at straight end and tape flap firmly to last cup. On each 4″ × 3¾″ piece of poster board, measure a 2″ square in the right corner and cut out. Then cut a triangle out of the middle of the bottom right side for toes, as in picture. Round off top corners with scissors. Attach legs to body cups by paper fasteners. Attach two legs, one on each side, to last cup of body and two legs to first cup. Paint yellow and orange spots on alllgator. Staple the ribbon or string to the top of the jaw cup, so you can tie up your alligator.

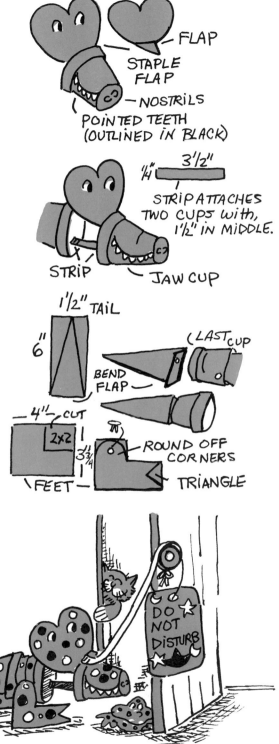

FLAP

STAPLE FLAP

NOSTRILS

POINTED TEETH (OUTLINED IN BLACK)

¼″ 3½″

STRIP ATTACHES TWO CUPS with, 1½″ IN MIDDLE.

STRIP

JAW CUP

1½″ TAIL

6″

BEND FLAP

(LAST CUP

4″ CUT

2x2

3¾″

FEET

ROUND OFF CORNERS

TRIANGLE

DO NOT DISTURB

25

PERCIVAL, THE FIRE-BREATHING DRAGON

Long ago in medieval days, dragons roamed the countryside. The dragon that the Little Witch and Goblin make is called Percival and he is very friendly. He will guard your room when you aren't at home.

You need: a tissue box (size that holds 200 tissues), one 6½" × 4½", one 9" × 5", one 3¼" × 3¼", one 7" × 2¾", and two 1¼" × 2¼" pieces of poster board painted purple, enough pieces of purple construction paper to cover the box, one 8" × 3", and two 8" × 4¾ pieces of poster board painted pink, four 4" × 4" pieces of poster board painted green, one 4" × 3" piece of red crepe paper, 40" string, paper fasteners, ruler, glue, stapler.

STAPLE STRING ENDS TO SIDES

6½

4½

EARS 1¼

2¼

3¼ (2 MOUNDS

FLAPS

7"

3¼

1½"

FLAPS

FLAP

GLUE

GLUE HEAD (3" ONLY) TO BOX.

Make sure all the painted parts are dry before you start. Turn box upside down, so opening is on the bottom. Cover the top and all four sides of box with purple construction paper cut to fit. Staple ends of 40" string to each side of box. Round off top corners on the 6½" × 4½" piece to look like a mound. Draw an ear on each 2¼" × 1¼" piece. Cut out. Staple to top of mound, as in picture. Glue about 3" of mound to front of box for head. Paint two yellow eyes outlined in black and with black pupils, 1" down from top of mound. Draw two mounds on top of the 3¼" × 3¼" piece of poster board. Cut out. Bend a 1½" flap at each end of the 7" × 2¾" piece. Glue or staple one flap to the center of the piece with two mounds, and attach the other flap to the center of the head mound. Draw two nostrils at end of nose and a curved mouth on head.

Measure 4″ in from one end on the top of each 8″ × 4¾″ piece of poster board. From dot draw a diagonal line to each corner to make a large triangle. Cut out on lines, then cut small scallops all along the bottom, as in picture. These are the wings. Bend a flap at the tip of each wing and tape or staple wings by flaps to sides of box, one wing to each side.

Cut a 2″ × 2″ square out of one top corner on each 4″ × 4″ piece of poster board. Then round off top corners. On long end of each foot, cut two triangle shapes out for toes. Make a tiny hole at top of each leg. Have an adult make four more holes, one at each corner of box, 1½″ from the edge and 1½″ up from the bottom. Attach legs to the box with paper fasteners through the holes. Measure off a 1″ flap down entire width of the 8″ × 3″ piece of poster board. Draw scallops all along top of flap. Cut out on lines. Bend flap and glue it along top of Dragon's back. Draw a crescent-moon shape on the 9″ × 5″ piece of poster board. Draw scallops along top and cut out. Form a flap by bending and tape flap securely to back of box. Bunch up the 4″ × 3″ red crepe and staple it below nostrils to look like fire. Paint spots on Dragon. Hang him up.

PINOCCHIO (Backpack puppet doll)

Geppetto, a modest man, carved a puppet out of wood and called him Pinocchio. Being very mischievous, Pinocchio ran away from home and got into a lot of trouble. At one point his nose grew every time he told a lie. When he returned home and promised to be good, a kind fairy with blue hair turned him into a real boy. The Little Witch and Goblin make a Pinocchio puppet doll that looks almost like the one Geppetto carved out of wood.

You need: an empty 16-oz. sugar box or similar-size box, construction paper cut to fit it, a 3½″ × 3½″ piece of white poster board, one 4″ × 4″ piece of yellow construction paper, two 6″ × 1″, four 4″ × 1″ strips of cardboard painted yellow, two 1″ × 1″ pieces of cardboard painted green, paper fasteners, stapler, ruler, paints, and 30″ of string.

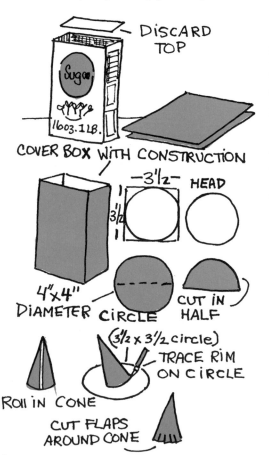

COVER BOX WITH CONSTRUCTION

— DISCARD TOP

—3½— HEAD

4″×4″ DIAMETER CIRCLE

CUT IN HALF

(3½ x 3½ circle) TRACE RIM ON CIRCLE

ROll IN CONE

CUT FLAPS AROUND CONE

Cut away the top flap on the sugar box, so top is entirely open. Trace the sides, back, and front of box on colored construction paper for Pinocchio's body. Cut out pieces and glue to cover box. Draw a full circle on the 3½″ × 3½″ piece of poster board and cut out. Cut a 4″ diameter circle out of yellow construction paper. Cut circle in half and roll one half into a narrow cone. Tape seam securely closed for nose. Trace the rim of the cone in the center of the 3½″ × 3½″ piece of white poster board. Cut out a small circle. Cut tiny flaps all around rim of cone. Slip cone through circle.

Tape flaps down securely. Staple the other yellow half circle to top of Pinocchio's head for hat. Staple ¾″ of Pinocchio's chin to top of sugar box. Use paper fasteners to attach Pinocchio's 6″ × 1″ arms to sides of sugar box. Attach arms about 1″ down from top. Ask an adult to punch tiny holes for you in the box. You need one hole on each side of box, 1″ up from bottom. Make another hole at top of each 4″ × 1″ leg. Attach top halves of legs to sides of box with paper fasteners through the holes. Then attach bottom 4″ × 1″ halves of legs to top parts in the same way. Draw circles on each 1″ × 1″ piece of cardboard and cut out. Staple to ends of arms for hands. Bend Pinocchio's legs so he can sit. Paint red or green boots on his feet, stars, and polka dots on his sugar-box body and stripes on hat. Store small items like a deck of cards in his backpack. Staple one end of a 30″ string to each shoulder. Hang him up, if you like.

FROG PRINCE

The Frog Prince was once a real prince, but a wicked witch turned him into a frog. He is made with methods and materials similar to Pinocchio.

You need: an empty 16-oz. sugar box, one 4½″ × 3½″, two 5½″ × 1″, two 6½″ × 1″ pieces of cardboard painted green, four 2½″ × 2″ pieces of orange construction paper, two 1¾″ × 1¼″ pieces of white poster board, one 3½″ × 3½″ piece of cardboard painted yellow, paper fasteners, stapler, ruler, and paints.

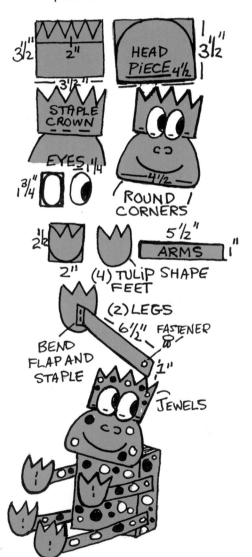

Cut away 2″ off entire top of sugar box. Cover box with green construction paper glued to fit it. Draw a pencil line across the 3½″ × 3½″ piece of yellow cardboard, 2″ from the edge. From line draw 5 crown points, as in picture. Cut out crown. Draw a half-circle-shaped head on the 4½″ × 3½″ piece of green cardboard. Cut out. Staple bottom of crown to top of half-circle head. Round off pointed corners. Paint nostrils and a frog grin. Draw an eye on each 1¾″ × 1¼″ piece of white poster board. Cut out. Paint black pupils. Staple bottom edge of eyes to top of head in front of the crown. Staple bottom of frog's head to top of box. Draw a tulip shape on each 2½″ × 2″ piece of orange construction paper. Cut out. Bend a ¼″ flap on each 5½″ × 1″ arm strip and each 6½″ × 1″ leg strip. Staple flaps to back of tulip shapes. Attach arms and legs with paper fasteners, as you did Pinocchio. Paint orange spots on frog.

STORYBOOK BOTTLE DOLLS

The Little Witch's Grandmother taught her how to make dolls from the bottles she collects. The Little Witch makes a Red Riding Hood doll, Goldilocks, and Merlin the Magician. If you use your imagination you can make many other dolls.

You need: an empty 10- or 12-oz. soda or beer bottle (make sure the rim is not chipped), a long pencil (about 7″), a 2½″ diameter styrofoam ball, a nylon sock, 7½″ × 8″, 10″ × 5½″, and 6½″ × 6½″ pieces of red cloth, two 3½″ × 1″ pieces of white poster board, strips of black crepe paper or yarn, four 4″ pieces, one 10″ piece, and a 16″ piece of ribbon, yellow construction paper, ruler, scissors, cement glue, stapler, and paints.

Stick the point of the pencil into the center of the styrofoam ball to a depth of about 1″. Don't stick yourself! Spread a layer of cement glue all around the mouth of the bottle. Insert free end of pencil into bottle and press ball down on glued rim to attach head to body. Hold head in place a few minutes to set glue and then let dry for about 45 minutes. When dry, gently pull nylon sock over head and down onto bottle. Be careful not to pull head off! Tie a 10″ ribbon around doll's neck to hold sock in place. Trim excess sock at bottom of bottle.

Cut tiny circles out of yellow construction paper and glue to doll's head for eyes and nose. Paint on pupils, eyebrows, and a red smile. Start gluing on the hair. You will need at least 30 to 35 ¼" × 4" strips of black crepe paper or yarn. Starting at top and middle of head, spread glue on about 1" of each 4" strip and stick glued part to head all around sides and back.

To make dress, open the 7½" × 8" piece of material and staple a 16" ribbon across top, as in picture, so you will have nearly 4" of ribbon extending from each side. Fit dress around doll and tie ribbon in back of neck, as in picture. Staple the arms. Pinch a bit of the dress at each side with your fingers and staple a 3½" × 1" piece of poster board to each side, slanting downwards. Round off other end with scissors and cut out a thumb shape.

To make cape, open the 6½" × 6½" piece of red cloth. Use red crepe paper if you can't find red cloth. Draw a full circle on the piece with a marker or round off the edges to form a circle. In the middle of the circle, draw a smaller 2" diameter circle and cut it out. (Helpful hint: trace around an upside down cereal bowl and a water glass or bottle to make circles.) Cut a slit from inner circle to edge of outer circle. Staple a 4″ ribbon to each side of opening on cape. Fit cape around doll's shoulders and tie closed.

To make hood, measure 5″ in from bottom of the 10″ × 5½″ piece of red cloth. Mark dot and draw a diagonal line from dot to each corner. Cut out triangle on lines and staple a 4″ ribbon at each pointed end. Drape the hood over Red Riding Hood's head and tie ribbons under chin. Doll can stand on your dresser.

To make Goldilocks, follow directions for Red Riding Hood, but use materials of different colors and make her hair of yellow yarn or crepe paper strips. She can play with the Three Country Bears on page 15. If you want to make Merlin the Magician, give him hair and a beard of cotton, a blue gown and cape. Glue stars to his outfit.

To make hat, cut a 6″ × 3″ half-circle out of construction paper, roll into a cone and tape seam shut. Glue stars and moons to it and place on head.

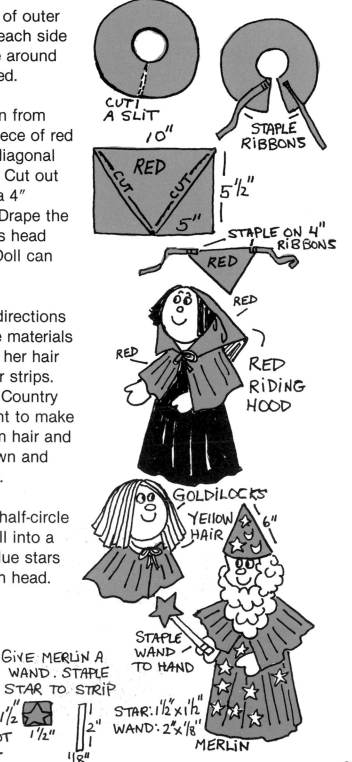

CUT A SLIT
10″
STAPLE RIBBONS
RED
CUT   CUT
5½″
5″
STAPLE ON 4″ RIBBONS
RED
RED
RED
RED RIDING HOOD
GOLDILOCKS
YELLOW HAIR
6″
STAPLE WAND TO HAND
MERLIN

6″
3″
HALF CIRCLE FOR HAT
CONE
DRAW AND CUT STAR OUT.
1½″
1½″
GIVE MERLIN A WAND. STAPLE A STAR TO STRIP
1″
2″
1″
1/8″
STAR: 1½″ × 1½″
WAND: 2″ × 1/8″

LITTLE WITCH ROADSTER

This Little Witch Roadster looks just like the real car that the Little Witch and her family ride around in.

You need: one 16″ × 10½″, one 4½″ × 3½″ and one 7″ × 2″ piece of cardboard painted orange; one 1½″ × 1½″ and four 3″ × 3″ pieces of cardboard painted black; one 2″ × 2″, one 1½″ × ¼″ piece of cardboard painted yellow; one 2″ × 2½″ piece of yellow or gray construction paper, masking tape, glue, ruler, paper fasteners, scissors, and paints.

Cut a 3″ × 3″ square out of each corner of the 16″ × 10½″ cardboard. Crease and bend flaps, as illustrated, to form a box. Close corner seams with masking tape. Measure 3″ in from each corner of box and cut out a 2″ × 1½″ rectangle to make four door areas. Draw a full circle on each 3″ × 3″ piece and cut out. Punch a tiny hole in the middle of each circle. The Little Witch lets her mother make all the holes through cardboard. Make four more holes at each end of box, about ¾″ in from the corners and ½″ up from the bottoms. Insert a paper fastener through the hole in each wheel and attach a wheel through each hole in box.

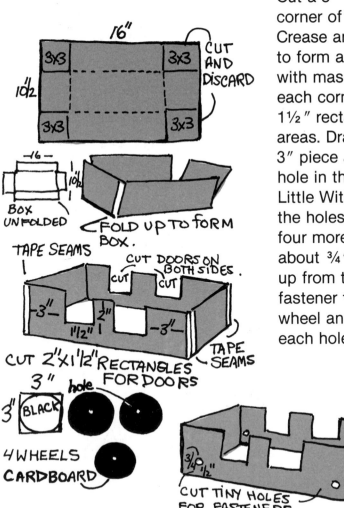

16″

3×3 3×3

CUT AND DISCARD

10½″

3×3 3×3

—16—

10½″

BOX UNFOLDED

FOLD UP TO FORM BOX.

TAPE SEAMS

CUT DOORS ON BOTH SIDES.
CUT CUT

—3″— 2″ —3″—
1½″

CUT 2″X1½″ RECTANGLES FOR DOORS

TAPE SEAMS

3″ hole

3″ BLACK

4 WHEELS CARDBOARD

¾″ ½″

CUT TINY HOLES FOR FASTENERS.

34

Place the 4½" × 3½" piece of orange cardboard over the top of one end of the box to make the front hood. Tape sides and front down to box. Paint taped seams orange. The hood will extend over the dashboard. Glue the 2" × 2½" grille to front of roadster. Paint crisscross lines on it. Draw a sailboat-shaped witch's hat on the 1½" × 1½" piece of cardboard and cut it out. Glue bottom half to top of grille as a hood ornament.

Draw a circle on 2" × 2" cardboard. Cut out for steering wheel. Cut a ¼" slit in the middle. Bend a ¼" flap on the 1½" × ¼" black cardboard strip and insert flap through slit in steering wheel and tape it down. Tape other end of black steering column under front of hood, as in picture. Paint spokes on steering wheel.

To make seat, measure 1½" from each end of 7" × 2" strip and bend into flaps to look like a bench. Place it in the roadster and tape or attach flaps to each side of car. Paint the words LITTLE WITCH ROADSTER on the back of your car and paint on a license plate that says WITCH 1. Ghosts ride in the roadster all the time, but you cannot see them.

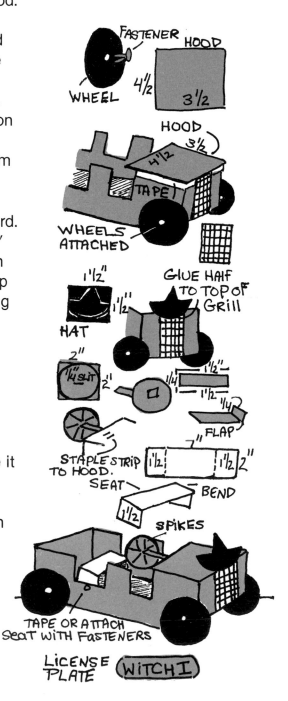

TIN WOODMAN

In the story, *The Wizard of Oz*, the Tin Woodman goes to ask the great Oz for a heart. The Little Witch makes Tin Woodman and gives him a heart.

You need: a toilet-paper tube, two 3½″ × ½″ and two 4½″ × ½″ pieces of cardboard painted gray or silver, a thin 2″ stick, two 2½″ × 1½″ pieces of cardboard painted black, 1″ × 1″ piece of red construction paper, and two 1″ × 1″ pieces of yellow construction paper, paints, stapler, ruler, white glue, paper fasteners, scissors, 7″ × 7″ square of aluminum foil, and a 2½″-diameter styrofoam ball.

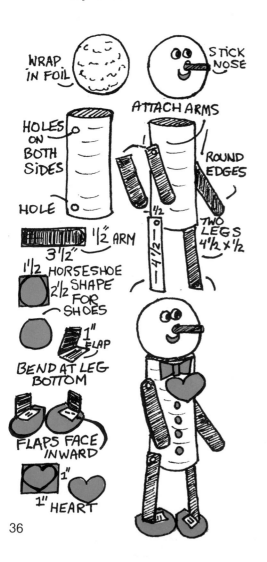

WRAP IN FOIL

STICK NOSE

ATTACH ARMS

HOLES ON BOTH SIDES

ROUND EDGES

HOLE

½

½ ARM

3½″

TWO LEGS 4½ × ½

4½

1½ HORSESHOE SHAPE FOR SHOES

2½

1″ FLAP

BEND AT LEG BOTTOM

FLAPS FACE INWARD

1″ HEART

1″

Cover the ball with the aluminum foil. Cut two dime-size eyes out of yellow construction paper and paint on black pupils. Glue eyes to ball. Insert stick into ball to a depth of about ½″ to make a nose. Paint nose gray. Cut out a small, red, smiling mouth from construction paper and glue below nose. Make tiny holes on each side of toilet-paper cylinder, about 1½″ down from top and ¾″ up from bottom. Use paper fasteners to attach the 4½″ × ½″ legs to bottom holes and shorter arms to top holes. Draw a horseshoe shape on each 2½″ × 1½″ piece of black cardboard and cut out. Bend a 1″ flap inward on each leg bottom. Staple flaps into horseshoes. Spread a layer of glue all around top rim of cylinder and bottom of ball. Glue ball to cylinder and hold in place to set glue, and then put aside to dry. Paint a bow and buttons on cylinder. Draw a heart on 1″ × 1″ red paper. Glue to cylinder, as in picture.

RALPH THE REVOLVING BOY ROBOT

The Little Witch and Goblin designed a toy robot that is very easy to make. You can name your robot anything you like. It does not have to be Ralph.

You need: three small 1-oz. cereal boxes from variety packs, two 4½″ × ¾″ strips of cardboard painted green, two 2″ × 1″ pieces of cardboard painted red, construction paper in various colors, white glue, ruler, paints, paper fastener.

When you empty the cereal boxes, try to keep the lids as neat as possible. Paint each box a different color. Put the paint on thick. You may need three coats and it will take a day to dry. When paint is dry, stand two boxes up sideways. Ask an adult to punch a hole in top center of one box and bottom center of the other. Attach the two boxes together by putting paper fastener through holes. Tape all the open box lids down. Round off one end of each 2″ × 1″ piece of cardboard with scissor and tape pieces under bottom box to serve as feet. Round off one end of each 4½″ × ¾″ strip of cardboard to make arms. Glue flat end of each arm to sides (lids closed) of middle box.

Cut several dime-sized pieces of construction paper in different colors and glue to boxes as control buttons. Glue the third box (head) to top of middle box (lengthways, not sideways). Glue circles to head for eyes, nose, and mouth. Let glue on head set and dry. Body revolves in a circle.

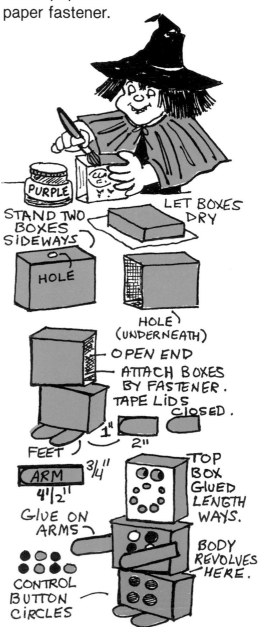

PURPLE

LET BOXES
DRY

STAND TWO
BOXES
SIDEWAYS

HOLE

HOLE
(UNDERNEATH)

OPEN END

ATTACH BOXES
BY FASTENER.
TAPE LIDS
CLOSED.

FEET

1″

2″

ARM   ¾″
4′|2″
GLUE ON
ARMS

TOP
BOX
GLUED
LENGTH
WAYS.

BODY
REVOLVES
HERE.

CONTROL
BUTTON
CIRCLES

DUCK WEATHER (Counting Board Game)

The Little Witch teaches her younger sister how to count from 1–10 with this board game. This also makes a nice gift for a little friend. The duck's wing points to the rain clouds above and puddles below.

You need: one 16″ × 16″ piece and one 7″ × 3½″ piece of white poster board, one 4″ × 8″, one 3½″ × 3½″ piece of yellow construction paper, two 3″ × 2½″, one 1½″ × 2½″ pieces of orange construction paper, rubber cement glue, scissors, ruler, paper fastener, stapler, paints, marker.

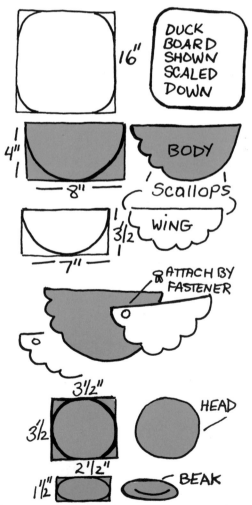

16″

DUCK BOARD SHOWN SCALED DOWN

4″

8″

BODY

Scallops

3/2

WING

7″

ATTACH BY FASTENER

3½″

3/2

2½″

1½″

HEAD

BEAK

Round off corners on the 16″ × 16″ piece with scissors. Draw a half-circle that touches edges on the 4″ × 8″ piece. Cut out. Cut three scallops at one end. Draw a half-circle on the 3½″ × 7″ piece and cut out. Cut scallops all along curve for wing, as illustrated. Measure 1½″ down from top and ¾″ in from unscalloped side of 4″ × 8″ half-circle body and make a small hole for a paper fastener. Measure ½″ from top corner of the 3½″ × 7″ half-circle wing and make another tiny hole. Attach wing to body with paper fastener through holes to make a movable wing.

Draw a full circle on the 3½″ × 3½″ piece of construction paper and cut out for head. Draw an oval on the 1½″ × 2½″ piece of orange construction paper and cut out for beak. Look at illustration. Staple oval to circle and paint a curved line across it to make a mouth. Paint on two dime-sized eyes with black pupils. Staple head to unscalloped corner of body, about 1″ down from top. Draw webbed foot on each 2½″ × 3″ piece and cut out. Staple feet to bottom of duck's body, one in front, one in back, as in picture.

Spread a layer of rubber cement over back of duck, but not on wing. Glue duck to center of 16″ × 16″ board. Press duck in place on board. When glue dries, roll away excess. Use marker to print DUCK WEATHER COUNTING GAME in ½″ letters at the top of your board. Starting at top right, outline five cloud shapes, each about 2″ × 1½″ circling the edge of the board, as illustrated. Then outline five wider puddles in a row along bottom of board. Paint puddles gray. Print the numbers 1–5 in the clouds and 6–10 in the puddles (after gray paint is dry). Paint green grass with colored flowers next to duck, a blue sky around duck and white clouds, and a yellow sun, if you like. Move duck's wing so it will point to a number in a cloud or puddle. This can be used to teach small children to identify numbers.

OSCAR THE OWL'S TELL-THE-TIME CLOCK

The Goblin made a clock modeled after his pet owl Oscar. You can show small children how to tell time with it. The little hand points to the hour and the big hand to the minutes.

You need: two 8″ × 8″ pieces of cardboard painted orange, two 2″ × 1½″, two 2½″ × 4″, one 2½″ × 1″, and one 2″ × 1″ pieces of yellow construction paper, paper fastener, stapler, ruler, and paints.

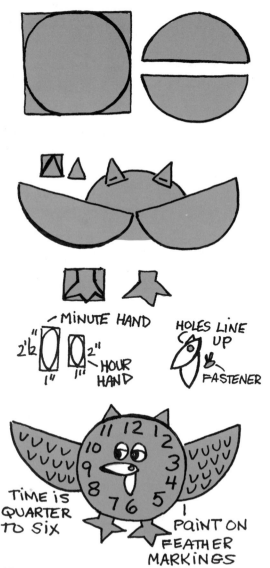

MINUTE HAND

2½″ HOUR HAND 1″ 1″ 2″

HOLES LINE UP
FASTENER

TIME IS QUARTER TO SIX

PAINT ON FEATHER MARKINGS

Draw the full circle on each 8″ × 8″ square and cut out. Cut one circle in half to make two wings. Staple one end of each wing to to the back of the circle. Draw a triangle on each 2″ × 1½″ piece of cardboard and cut out for ears. Staple ears to top of circle. Draw claw feet on the 2½″ × 4″ pieces of cardboard, cut out, and staple to bottom of circle. To make a minute hand, draw a long oval on the 2½″ × 1″ piece of construction paper, and for the hour hand, draw an oval on the 2″ × 1″ piece of construction paper. Cut out.

Paint two yellow eyes 2½″ down from top of head. Make each eye 1½″ long and 1″ wide, and outline eyes in black. Paint numbers around the clock, as in picture. Make a tiny hole in center of clock and at tip of each hand of clock. Put the hands together, so holes line up, and poke a paper fastener through the holes in the hands and through the hole in the clock. You will now have movable hands on your Oscar the Owl Tell-the-Time Clock.

40

HOLIDAY AND SEASONAL TOYS

Toy Workshop, Party, and Sale

MONSTER MITTS OR CLAW PAWS

The Little Witch and her friend the Goblin have a lot of fun making Monster Mitts (also known as Claw Paws) for Halloween or any time of the year. When a friend comes to your door, open it slightly and stick out a horrible hairy paw. You can probably think of many other ways to play with Monster Mitts.

You need: four pieces of 9″ × 12″ craft felt of any color you like for paws, ten ½″ × 1″ pieces of poster board of some good color (like green) for claws, a sheet of construction paper, scissors, ruler, stapler, white glue, marker, and paints.

Lay your hand and wrist on a piece of craft felt spread out on a table or flat surface. Trace around your fingers with a marker, but draw each finger bigger than your own. Leave about a ½″ border around each finger. Trace about halfway down each finger, giving each a thick rounded shape.

Cut out pattern for fat hand you have traced. Trace the hand on another piece of felt and cut that out, also. Staple the hand shapes together all around, except at bottom. Be sure staples are closed, so you don't scratch yourself. You can wear a pair of regular gloves under the Monster Mitts to make them thick and scary. Trace your other hand on the remaining two pieces of craft felt. Cut out and staple hand shapes together, just as you did for your first Mitt. Paint spots on paws or glue on circles cut out of construction paper. Glue small strips of yarn to backs of paws to look like hair or fur. Draw a triangle shape on each ½″ × 1″ piece of poster board and cut out. Staple one of these claws to each fingertip.

HAUNTED CASTLE (With Ice-Cream Stick Ghosts)

The Little Witch likes to make a haunted castle to play with at Halloween or any time of the year. You can have fun making a castle for yourself and your friends to play with.

You need: two paper-towel cylinders painted pink or blue, one 9″ × 7″ piece of cardboard painted gray or red, two 6″ × 3″ pieces of yellow construction paper, two 2″ × 1″ pieces of pink construction paper, four 2½″ × 4″ pieces of white poster board, four ice-cream sticks or coffee stirrers, toothpicks, scissors, ruler, glue, paints.

Cut out two arch-shaped windows, on the upper half of each cardboard tube. Make each window about 2″ high and 1″ wide. Measure off nine 1″ squares along top of 9″ × 7″ cardboard. Cut out only every other square, so the first and last squares are cut out. Next, cut a slit 6″ long in each cardboard tube, starting on the side away from the windows. Insert wall through each slit to attach wall to towers.

Draw a half circle on each 6″ × 3″ piece of construction paper and cut out. Roll half circles into cones and tape seams closed. Place over towers as roofs. Draw a fat, skinny, or funny ghost on each 2½″ × 4″ piece of poster board and glue to the top of an ice-cream stick. Insert sticks through tower windows, so ghosts float outside. Cut flags out of 2″ × 1″ pieces of pink construction paper and glue to tops of toothpicks. Insert toothpicks in tops of towers. Paint marks on walls to look like blocks of stone.

POTATO ELVES

The Little Witch and Goblin make elves out of potatoes. Elves are friendly little people who live in the woods and in secret places in houses. Santa's helpers in his toyshop at the north pole are elves. You can easily make some of your own elves for Christmas or any time of year. Make as many elves as you like.

For each elf, you need: a small or medium, unpeeled raw potato, four small 2½ " to 3" twigs or ice-cream sticks for arms and legs, one 5" × 2½ " piece of colored construction paper, acorn caps, gumdrops, toothpicks, cotton batting, white glue, paints.

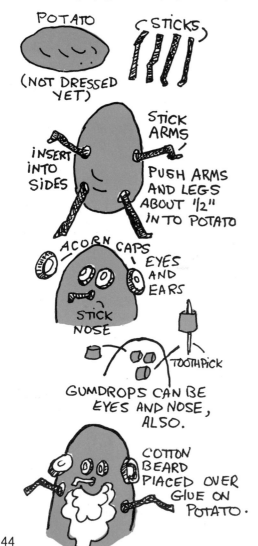

POTATO

(NOT DRESSED YET)

(STICKS)

STICK ARMS

INSERT INTO SIDES

PUSH ARMS AND LEGS ABOUT ½" INTO POTATO

ACORN CAPS

EYES AND EARS

STICK NOSE

TOOTHPICK

GUMDROPS CAN BE EYES AND NOSE, ALSO.

COTTON BEARD PLACED OVER GLUE ON POTATO.

Wash the potato and let it dry. Find four twigs for arms and legs, each about 2½ " to 3" long. They can be crooked and bent. You can break off pieces from larger dead branches, or use tongue depressors or ice-cream sticks from the crafts store. Insert a stick for an arm on each side of the potato and one stick on each side for legs. You may need an adult to help make a small hole in the potato with a knife for each arm and leg. You can paint the arms and legs, if you like. Elf eyes can be painted on, or glue on two acorn caps. Ears can also be of acorn caps. Small gumdrops inserted into potato with toothpicks make nice eyes. Make elf noses of small twigs or gumdrops on toothpicks. Paint on a red mouth and paint noses red or green. Glue cotton under mouth to make a long or short beard.

For elf hat, draw a half circle on the 5″ × 2½″ piece of construction paper (red or green if it is for Christmas). Cut out half circle and roll it into a cone. Tape seam closed. Hat can be made wider if a wider hat is needed for a big head. Paint stars and moons on hat.

Elf may not stand unless you find sticks the same size for both legs and insert them directly at sides of potato. You can prop elf up against something if you need to. Stick each leg in a jumbo gumdrop to make snow shoes, if you like. Glue two cardboard oval feet under potato and glue bottoms of feet to two ice cream sticks if you want an elf on skis.

How many funny elves, gnomes, and goblins can you think up?

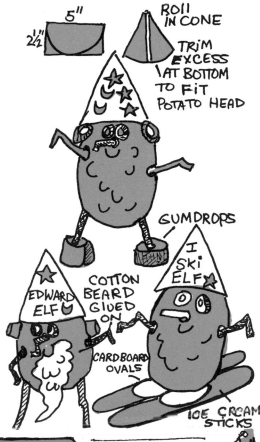

TOY WORKSHOP PARTY AND SALE

At the end of a busy season, the Little Witch and Goblin have a toy workshop party and sale. To have a toy sale you need some space and a few tables. The sale can be held in your toy workshop, outside on a picnic table, on your porch, or wherever you can get space. Perhaps you can have a toy sale at school. Ask your teacher. The money earned can go toward school events, like a trip to a museum, or to a favorite charity, like an animal fund. The toy workshop party is open to the public, but the Little Witch and Goblin send out a few invitations to special friends a week before the sale. They make Pinocchio-nose invitations and you can, too.

For each invitation you need: one 12″ × 1½″ piece of yellow construction paper, one 4″ × 4″ piece of beige or light-color construction paper, one 4¼″ × 2½″ piece of green construction paper, stapler, ruler, scissors, marker and paints.

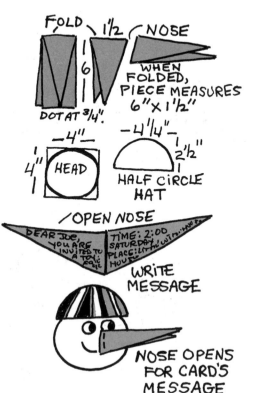

FOLD ⟋ 1½ ⟋ NOSE

6

WHEN FOLDED, PIECE MEASURES 6″ × 1½″

DOT AT ¾″.

4″ × 4″

4″ HEAD

4¼″ — 2½″

HALF CIRCLE HAT

⟋ OPEN NOSE

DEAR JOE, YOU ARE INVITED TO A TOY SALE

TIME: 2:00 SATURDAY PLACE: LITTLE WITCH HOUSE

WRITE MESSAGE

NOSE OPENS FOR CARD'S MESSAGE

Fold the 12″ × 1½″ piece of construction paper in half the long way. Make a dot in the center of the bottom edge and then draw a diagonal line up to each corner. Cut along lines through both pieces up to the fold, as in picture. Draw a full circle on the 4″ × 4″ piece of construction paper and cut out. Draw a half circle on the 4¼″ × 2½″ piece of construction paper. Cut out and staple to top of circle to serve as a hat. Staple nose sideways to circle by the folded end. Paint on eyes and mouth. Paint stripes on Pinocchio's hat. Open nose and write message.

Dear Joe,
You are invited to a toy sale and party.
Time: 2:00 Saturday, Place: Little
Witch's house.

DISPLAYING AND SELLING YOUR TOYS

Choose the toys you want to sell. The smaller toys like Tin Woodman, Robot, Lion Cubs, and Baby Bear are easier to make and may sell faster. The Little Witch and Goblin have a table for their sale items and a special display table for toys they want to exhibit, but that are not for sale. Keep a note pad and pencil handy. If someone sees a toy they like, they can order it from the workshop and you can make it for them another day.

Here is what the Little Witch and Goblin charge for some of their toys: Leo the Leopard, and Leslie the Lion, 50¢ each. They charge 75¢ for a Unicorn, 50¢ for a Country Bear, 25¢ for a Baby Bear, 60¢ for a Frog Prince, 35¢ for a Tin Woodman, 40¢ for a Revolving Robot. You can charge whatever you like. Exceptionally fine toys should be 75¢ to $1.00.

Party refreshments are on the next page.

PINOCCHIO COOKIES

The Little Witch and Goblin serve their customers and guests Pinocchio Cookies and milk, fruit punch, or soda. An adult should always help you use the oven.

For cookies you need:

½ cup melted butter
1 egg
1 cup all-purpose flour

⅓ cup sugar
1 tsp. vanilla extract

Mix butter, egg, sugar, and vanilla together thoroughly in a large bowl. Add the flour and mix well. Knead dough with your hands and make it into a large ball. Then shape the dough into several small balls, each about 1″ in diameter. Flatten with your hand to form cookie and bake on a greased cookie sheet at 375° for 12 minutes, or until edges are slightly brown (makes 2 to 2½ dozen cookies).

When cookies have cooled, spread a thin layer of creamy peanut butter over each. Place two candy drops on each cookie for eyes. Mouth can be made of raisins or candies. Ask an adult to cut several very thin, raw carrot sticks, each about 1″ long. Put carrot stick sideways below eyes on each cookie to make a long nose. Scatter sprinkles on top part of cookie to look like Pinocchio's hat. Serve milk or punch in paper cups. Keep napkins handy.